Let's Explore
Sound

by Walt K. Moon

BUMBA BOOKS™

LERNER PUBLICATIONS ◆ MINNEAPOLIS

Note to Educators:

Throughout this book, you'll find critical thinking questions. These can be used to engage young readers in thinking critically about the topic and in using the text and photos to do so.

Lerner Publications Company
A division of Lerner Publishing Group, Inc.
241 First Avenue North
Minneapolis, MN 55401 USA

For reading levels and more information, look up this title at www.lernerbooks.com.

Library of Congress Cataloging-in-Publication Data

Names: Moon, Walt K., author.
Title: Let's explore sound / by Walt K. Moon.
Description: Minneapolis : Lerner Publications, [2018] | Series: Bumba books.
  A first look at physical science | Audience: Ages 4–7. | Audience:
  K to Grade 3. | Includes bibliographical references and index.
Identifiers: LCCN 2017019800 (print) | LCCN 2017024752 (ebook) | ISBN
  9781512482775 (eb pdf) | ISBN 9781512482713 (lb : alk. paper) | ISBN
  9781541510869 (pb : alk. paper)
Subjects: LCSH: Sound—Juvenile literature.
Classification: LCC QC225.5 (ebook) | LCC QC225.5 .M63 2018 (print) | DDC
  534—dc23

LC record available at https://lccn.loc.gov/2017019800

Manufactured in the United States of America
1 – CG – 12/31/17

LERNER
SOURCE™

Expand learning beyond the printed book. Download free, complementary educational resources for this book from our website, www.lernerresource.com.

Table of Contents

What Is Sound?

Sound is everywhere.

Everything we hear is sound.

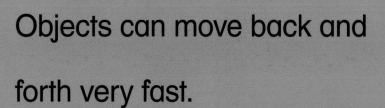

Objects can move back and forth very fast.

This makes the air around them vibrate.

We hear vibrations as sound.

Clapping makes noise. What other hand movements make sound?

Our ears hear the vibrations.

They send signals to the brain.

The brain knows vibrations as sound.

Our ears cannot hear all sounds.

Some things vibrate too quickly or too slowly.

Dogs may hear these sounds.

Do you think other animals can hear sounds humans cannot?

Music is made up of sounds.

Instruments make different notes.

Hitting a drum makes vibrations.

People make sounds.

Voices are important sounds.

They let us talk to one another.

People speak on phones.

Sound travels through devices.

Many objects make sounds.

Fans buzz quietly.

Vacuums hum loudly.

What other everyday objects make sounds?

Sounds fill our world.

Birds chirp.

Wind blows through trees.

What sounds do you hear

every day?

Picture Quiz

Which of these pictures shows something making a sound?

Picture Glossary

devices

pieces of equipment, such as telephones and headphones

instruments

objects that are used to make music

signals

messages that give information

vibrate

to move back and forth rapidly

23

Read More

Boothroyd, Jennifer. *Vibrations Make Sound.* Minneapolis: Lerner Publications, 2015.

Johnson, Robin. *What Are Sound Waves?* New York: Crabtree Publishing Company, 2014.

Pfeffer, Wendy. *Sounds All Around.* New York: HarperCollins, 2016.

Index

Photo Credits